I SAY PLEASE AND THANK YOU

LIFT-THE-FLAP MANNERS

by RACHEL ISADORA
& ROBIE ROGGE

Illustrated by
RACHEL ISADORA

HOLIDAY HOUSE · NEW YORK

T0035839

I say, "Hello," . . .

When I want a treat, I say . . .

And when I get a present, I say . . .

When I make a new friend, I say . . .

I farted. So I say . . .

If I step on someone's foot, I say . . .

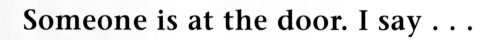

Someone is at the door. I say . . .

I say, "May I have a cupcake, please," . . .

If someone is in trouble, I say . . .

When someone comes back home,
we wave and say . . .

For Alex Kramer, who always knows his manners —R.I.

And my own thanks to Rachel Isadora —R.R.

Text copyright © 2021 by Rachel Isadora and Robie Rogge
Illustrations copyright © 2021 by Rachel Isadora

All Rights Reserved
HOLIDAY HOUSE is registered in the U.S. Patent and Trademark Office.
Printed and bound in June 2021 at Leo Paper, Heshan, China.
The artwork was created with pen, ink and watercolor.
www.holidayhouse.com
First Edition
1 3 5 7 9 10 8 6 4 2

Library of Congress Cataloging-in-Publication Data
Names: Isadora, Rachel, author. | Rogge, Robie, author.
Title: I say please and thank you : lift-the-flap manners / by Rachel
Isadora, Robie Rogge ; Illustrated by Rachel Isadora.
Description: First edition | New York, N.Y. : Holiday House, 2021.
Audience: Ages 2–5 | Audience: Grades K–1 | Summary: "Open the flaps for
a fun and friendly way to learn good manners!"—Provided by publisher.
Identifiers: LCCN 2021001572 | ISBN 9780823449194 (hardcover)
Subjects: LCSH: Etiquette for children and teenagers—Juvenile literature
Lift-the-flap books—Specimens. | Toy and movable books—Specimens. | Board books.
Classification: LCC BJ1857.C5 I83 2021 | DDC 395.1/22—dc23
LC record available at https://lccn.loc.gov/2021001572
ISBN: 978-0-8234-4919-4 (hardcover)